# Clouds!

Scott Harper

INFOMAX COMMON CORE READERS

Rosen Classroom™

New York

Published in 2014 by The Rosen Publishing Group, Inc.
29 East 21st Street, New York, NY 10010



Book Design: Jon D'Rozario

Photo Credits: Cover © Andrey tiky/Shutterstock.com; p. 5 Songchai W/Shutterstock.com; p. 7 (high) Steve Mann/Shutterstock.com; p. 7 (middle) Stacey Lynn Payne/Shutterstock.com; pp. 7, 15 (low) paul prescott/Shutterstock.com; p. 9 donvictorio/Shutterstock.com; p. 11 Lorelinka/Shutterstock.com; p. 13 (gray) Mona Makela/Shutterstock.com; p. 13 (white) Serg64/Shutterstock.com; p. 17 pictureguy/Shutterstock.com; p. 19 Katarzyna Mazurowska/Shutterstock.com; p. 21 Todd Shoemake/Shutterstock.com; p. 22 Vasaleks/Shutterstock.com.

ISBN: 978-1-4777-2284-8
6-pack ISBN: 978-1-4777-2285-5

Manufactured in the United States of America

CPSIA Compliance Information: Batch #CS13RC: For further information contact Rosen Publishing, New York, New York at 1-800-237-9932.

# Contents

# Making a Cloud

It's fun to look at clouds in the sky! Clouds are made of water, which goes into the air as a gas called water vapor. As the water vapor rises, it gets colder. This turns it back into a **liquid**. Then, the water sticks to dust in the air. This makes tiny drops of water called droplets. Clouds are made of many water droplets together.

Clouds may look different, but they're all made of water.

# How Are Clouds Formed?

water vapor rises in the air

▼

water vapor cools as it rises

▼

water vapor turns back into a liquid

▼

water sticks to dust to make droplets

▼

droplets come together to make clouds

Some clouds form higher in the sky than other clouds. The lowest clouds are often thick and dark. Rain and snow can come from these clouds. Clouds in the middle of the sky are made of liquid water droplets in the summer, but the droplets mix with ice in the winter. The highest clouds are made of ice.

Different types of clouds form in different parts of the sky.

high

middle

low

# High in the Sky

The clouds that form highest in the sky are called cirrus (SIHR-uhs) clouds. They're made of ice, which makes them very thin and white. These clouds don't produce rain, but they can tell us if rain is coming. If you see cirrus clouds, that means the weather is going to change. Some cirrus clouds show up before big storms, like **hurricanes**.

Have you seen a change in the weather lately? You probably saw cirrus clouds before it happened!

# Fluffy Clouds

Another kind of white cloud looks like a big ball of cotton. This is a cumulus (KYOO-myuh-luhs) cloud. You can see cumulus clouds on sunny days because they're fair-weather clouds. This means they don't bring rain or snow. Cumulus clouds look fluffy. Can you name other fluffy things you see around you?

Cumulus clouds can grow to be very tall!

# White Clouds, Gray Clouds

Cirrus clouds and cumulus clouds are white. What makes them this color? The sun shines through these clouds easily, and that lets us see every color of the rainbow in the sunlight. All those colors together look white to us. Other clouds are too thick for the sun to shine through. This makes them look gray.

What color are the clouds you see today? Is the light from the sun shining brightly, or is it too cloudy?

white

gray

# Rainy Days

Stratus (STRA-tuhs) clouds are a common kind of gray cloud. They cover the whole sky like a gray blanket! Stratus clouds can usually be seen very low in the sky, and they're very thick. Some stratus clouds produce **steady** and heavy rain, and some only produce light rain. This is called drizzle.

When it's cold enough, snow falls from some stratus clouds. Does it get cold enough where you live for these clouds to produce snow?

Rain also falls from a special kind of cumulus cloud. When a cumulus cloud grows very big, it becomes a cumulonimbus (kyoo-myuh-loh-NIHM-buhs) cloud. High winds make the top of the cloud flat. These clouds are storm clouds. They produce a lot of rain and snow. Sometimes, balls of ice fall from these clouds. This is called hail.

Cumulonimbus clouds are a sign of stormy weather. What kinds of stormy weather do you get where you live?

# Hard to See!

Certain kinds of clouds aren't seen very often. Fog is a kind of stratus cloud that touches the ground. Most fog is seen in the morning. When the air gets warmer during the day, the fog begins to rise up from the ground. Mountains and hills often have a lot of fog around them!

It's hard to see when there's a lot of fog. Have you ever had trouble seeing things because of the weather?

# Big Storms!

Green clouds are another **rare** kind of cloud. They produce strong storms. **Funnel** clouds also happen during strong storms. A funnel cloud is a sign of a tornado. This is a storm with very strong winds spinning in a circle. A tornado is a very **severe** storm. It's important to find a safe place to stay until the funnel cloud passes.

Where are some safe places you could go if there were a tornado near you?

# What's the Weather?

It's important to know what different types of clouds mean. Clouds tell us a lot about the weather. Looking at the clouds can tell you if it's going to be sunny or stormy. It can also tell you if the weather is going to change. What do the clouds outside your window look like today?

# Glossary

**funnel** (FUH-nuhl) Having a shape that is wide on top and narrow on the bottom.

**hurricane** (HUHR-uh-kayn) A storm with strong winds and heavy rain.

**liquid** (LIH-kwuhd) Something that flows freely like water.

**rare** (REHR) Not often.

**severe** (suh-VEER) Very strong.

**steady** (STEH-dee) Not stopping.

# Index